FRANK LLO...

photographs by
Alan Weintraub

2007 engagement
calendar ◆ ◆ ◆ ◆ ◆

Pomegranate

COLLECTION

Catalog No. V279
Published by Pomegranate Communications, Inc.
Box 808022, Petaluma CA 94975

This Frank Lloyd Wright Collection® product is authorized by the Frank Lloyd Wright Foundation,
Taliesin West, Scottsdale, Arizona, and has been developed with the cooperation of the Frank
Lloyd Wright Preservation Trust. A portion of the sales of this product supports the conservation
and education programs of these institutions. The Frank Lloyd Wright Home and Studio, Oak Park,
Illinois, is an historic site of the National Trust for Historic Preservation.

Available in Canada from Canadian Manda Group
165 Dufferin Street, Toronto, Ontario M6K 3H6

Available in the UK and mainland Europe from Pomegranate Europe Ltd.
Unit 1, Heathcote Business Centre, Hurlbutt Road, Warwick, Warwickshire CV34 6TD, UK

Available in Australia from Hardie Grant Books, 12 Claremont Street, South Yarra, Victoria 3141

Available in New Zealand from Southern Publishers Group, P.O. Box 8360, Symonds Street, Auckland

Available in the Far East from Julian Ashton, Ashton International Marketing Services
P.O. Box 298, Sevenoaks, Kent TN13 1WU, UK

Africa, Latin America, and the Middle East: info@pomegranate.com; 707-782-9000

Pomegranate publishes Frank Lloyd Wright's architectural and graphic work in three 2007 wall calendars,
jigsaw puzzles, books, notecards, postcards and books of postcards, address books, leather journals,
mousepads, magnets, bookmarks, posters, and a stationery set. For more information or to place an
order, please contact Pomegranate Communications, Inc.: 800-227-1428; www.pomegranate.com.

Designed by Shannon Lemme

Dates in color indicate federal holidays.
All astronomical data supplied in this calendar are expressed in Greenwich Mean Time (GMT).
Moon phases and American, Canadian, and UK holidays are noted.

● NEW MOON ☽ FIRST QUARTER ○ FULL MOON ☾ LAST QUARTER

Frank Lloyd Wright (1867–1959) changed the face of architecture. Well over a century since the completion of his earliest solo residential commission, we see his architectural principles expressed everywhere. They have so thoroughly become part of our architectural vocabulary that we risk taking them for granted—especially in cases where Wright's ideas were expropriated and misused by builders of cookie-cutter tract houses.

Those ideas certainly could not be taken for granted in the architect's lifetime: they were far too radical. From the first, he pushed the envelope of convention with his treatments of Shingle Style and Craftsman homes; given the opportunity, he moved beyond them into new designs involving new concepts and principles. Wright's Prairie houses of the early twentieth century broke loose from their boxy antecedents, responding to the flatness of their prairie surroundings with strong, daredevilishly cantilevered horizontals. His 1920s California houses demonstrated his evolving ideas about concrete block construction and integral ornament. His Usonian designs of the forties and fifties brought architectural excellence to people of modest means. And his masterworks—Fallingwater, Wingspread, Taliesin and Taliesin West, and many more—secured his place as the most important architect in American history.

Wright called his overarching theory "organic architecture": his buildings grew from the characteristics of the site, the natural materials to be found locally, and the structural shapes that would best answer the shapes of their surroundings. From his first building to his last, he continually experimented with materials and techniques, expanding and refining his architectural principles and imbuing his visions of modernism with the American qualities of independence and self-reliance. Amazingly prolific in designs, concepts, and writings, Wright was a true twentieth-century original.

2007

JANUARY

s	m	t	w	t	f	s
	1	2	3	4	5	6
7	8	9	10	11	12	13
14	15	16	17	18	19	20
21	22	23	24	25	26	27
28	29	30	31			

FEBRUARY

s	m	t	w	t	f	s
				1	2	3
4	5	6	7	8	9	10
11	12	13	14	15	16	17
18	19	20	21	22	23	24
25	26	27	28			

MARCH

s	m	t	w	t	f	s
				1	2	3
4	5	6	7	8	9	10
11	12	13	14	15	16	17
18	19	20	21	22	23	24
25	26	27	28	29	30	31

APRIL

s	m	t	w	t	f	s
1	2	3	4	5	6	7
8	9	10	11	12	13	14
15	16	17	18	19	20	21
22	23	24	25	26	27	28
29	30					

MAY

s	m	t	w	t	f	s
		1	2	3	4	5
6	7	8	9	10	11	12
13	14	15	16	17	18	19
20	21	22	23	24	25	26
27	28	29	30	31		

JUNE

s	m	t	w	t	f	s
					1	2
3	4	5	6	7	8	9
10	11	12	13	14	15	16
17	18	19	20	21	22	23
24	25	26	27	28	29	30

2007

JULY

s	m	t	w	t	f	s
1	2	3	4	5	6	7
8	9	10	11	12	13	14
15	16	17	18	19	20	21
22	23	24	25	26	27	28
29	30	31				

AUGUST

s	m	t	w	t	f	s
			1	2	3	4
5	6	7	8	9	10	11
12	13	14	15	16	17	18
19	20	21	22	23	24	25
26	27	28	29	30	31	

SEPTEMBER

s	m	t	w	t	f	s
						1
2	3	4	5	6	7	8
9	10	11	12	13	14	15
16	17	18	19	20	21	22
23/30	24	25	26	27	28	29

OCTOBER

s	m	t	w	t	f	s
	1	2	3	4	5	6
7	8	9	10	11	12	13
14	15	16	17	18	19	20
21	22	23	24	25	26	27
28	29	30	31			

NOVEMBER

s	m	t	w	t	f	s
				1	2	3
4	5	6	7	8	9	10
11	12	13	14	15	16	17
18	19	20	21	22	23	24
25	26	27	28	29	30	

DECEMBER

s	m	t	w	t	f	s
						1
2	3	4	5	6	7	8
9	10	11	12	13	14	15
16	17	18	19	20	21	22
23/30	24/31	25	26	27	28	29

I have, lifelong, been fighting the pull of the specious old box. I have had such a curious, controversial and interesting time doing it that I myself have become a controversial item. Suspicion is in order.

♦　♦　♦　Frank Lloyd Wright

Louis Penfield House (1953), Willoughby Hills, Ohio. Of modest height himself, Wright rose to the challenge of designing a home whose proportions would "look right" surrounding his 6'8" client. The interior doors, for instance, are 8' x 22".

JANUARY

SUNDAY	MONDAY	TUESDAY	WEDNESDAY	THURSDAY	FRIDAY	SATURDAY
	1	2	3 ○	4	5	6
7	8	9	10	11 ☾	12	13
14	15	16	17	18	19 ●	20
21	22	23	24	25 ☽	26	27
28	29	30	31			

JAN 1   NEW YEAR'S DAY
JAN 2   BANK HOLIDAY (SCOTLAND)
JAN 15 MARTIN LUTHER KING JR. DAY

JANUARY

monday

1 _____

tuesday

2 _____

wednesday

3 3 ○ _____

thursday

4 4 _____

friday

5 5 _____

saturday

6 6 _____

sunday

7 7 _____

JANUARY

monday
8 8

tuesday
9 9

wednesday
10 10

thursday
☾11 11

friday
12 12

saturday
13 13

sunday
14 14

s	m	t	w	t	f	s
	1	2	3	4	5	6
7	8	9	10	11	12	13
14	15	16	17	18	19	20
21	22	23	24	25	26	27
28	29	30	31			

JANUARY

*The old house must be thrown away entirely
and a new one, more fit to live in, conceived
in the spirit of organic architecture.*

◆   ◆   ◆   Frank Lloyd Wright

Frank Lloyd Wright Home and Studio (1889–1898), Oak Park, Illinois. Wright's shingle—the carved stone by the entrance to his first architecture studio—has his early logotype, a cross within a circle bounded by a square, in the lower right corner. He soon simplified it into the better-known square red "chop."

JANURY

JANUARY

MARTIN LUTHER KING JR. DAY

monday
15 · 15

tuesday
16 · 16

wednesday
17 · 17

thursday
18 · 18

● **friday**
19 · 19

saturday
20 · 20

sunday
21 · 21

s	m	t	w	t	f	s
	1	2	3	4	5	6
7	8	9	10	11	12	13
14	15	16	17	18	19	20
21	22	23	24	25	26	27
28	29	30	31			

JANUARY

Sidney Bazett House (1939), Hillsborough, California. Wright took a playful approach to the introduction of natural light into his buildings: he bounced it, redirected it, scattered it, and focused it in surprising places. The wall-less definition of interior spaces is another of Wright's favorite devices.

JANUARY

monday
22   22

tuesday
23   23

wednesday
24   24

thursday
☽25   25

friday
26   26

saturday
27   27

s	m	t	w	t	f	s
	1	2	3	4	5	6
7	8	9	10	11	12	13
14	15	16	17	18	19	20
21	22	23	24	25	26	27
28	29	30	31			

JANUARY

sunday
28   28

JAN/FEB

monday
29 29

tuesday
30 30

wednesday
31 31

thursday
32 1

friday
33 2 ○

saturday
34 3

sunday
35 4

FEBRUARY

SUNDAY	MONDAY	TUESDAY	WEDNESDAY	THURSDAY	FRIDAY	SATURDAY
				1	2 ○	3
4	5	6	7	8	9	10 ☾
11	12	13	14	15	16	17 ●
18	19	20	21	22	23	24 ☽
25	26	27	28			

FEB 12   LINCOLN'S BIRTHDAY
FEB 14   VALENTINE'S DAY
FEB 19   PRESIDENTS' DAY
FEB 21   ASH WEDNESDAY
FEB 22   WASHINGTON'S BIRTHDAY

Meyer May House (1908), Grand Rapids, Michigan. Strong horizontal planes and a generous overhanging roofline are characteristic of Wright's Prairie period. "A Home in a Prairie Town" was the architect's first published piece.

FEBRUARY

monday
5   36

tuesday
6   37

wednesday
7   38

thursday
8   39

friday
9   40

saturday
10   41

s	m	t	w	t	f	s
				1	2	3
4	5	6	7	8	9	10
11	12	13	14	15	16	17
18	19	20	21	22	23	24
25	26	27	28			

FEBRUARY

sunday
11   42

*Organic architecture calls for a chair which will
not look like an apparatus but instead be seen
as a gracious feature of its environment.*

◆   ◆   ◆   Frank Lloyd Wright

Karl A. Staley House (1950), North Madison, Ohio. Freestanding and built-in furniture defines spaces for conversation and dining. The glass facade faces Lake Erie.

FEBRUARY

LINCOLN'S BIRTHDAY

12   43

13   44

VALENTINE'S DAY

14   45

15   46

16   47

17   48

s	m	t	w	t	f	s
				1	2	3
4	5	6	7	8	9	10
11	12	13	14	15	16	17
18	19	20	21	22	23	24
25	26	27	28			

FEBRUARY

18   49

Terminal masses are most important as to form. Nature will show this to you in her own fabrications. Take good care of the terminals and the rest will take care of itself.

◆   ◆   ◆   Frank Lloyd Wright

Susan Lawrence Dana/Dana-Thomas House (1902–1904), Springfield, Illinois. As he explored the integration of structure and ornament, Wright's work after 1900 became simpler in form without sacrificing spatial complexity.

FEBRUARY

monday

19 50

PRESIDENTS' DAY

tuesday

20 51

wednesday

21 52

ASH WEDNESDAY

thursday

22 53

WASHINGTON'S BIRTHDAY

friday

23 54

saturday

☽24 55

sunday

25 56

s	m	t	w	t	f	s
				1	2	3
4	5	6	7	8	9	10
11	12	13	14	15	16	17
18	19	20	21	22	23	24
25	26	27	28			

FEBRUARY

FEB / MAR

monday
57 26

tuesday
58 27

wednesday
59 28

thursday
60 1

friday
61 2

saturday
62 3 ○   PURIM (BEGINS AT SUNSET)

sunday
63 4

MARCH

SUNDAY	MONDAY	TUESDAY	WEDNESDAY	THURSDAY	FRIDAY	SATURDAY
				1	2	3 ○
4	5	6	7	8	9	10
11	12 ☾	13	14	15	16	17
18	19 ●	20	21	22	23	24
25 ☽	26	27	28	29	30	31

MAR 3   PURIM (BEGINS AT SUNSET)
MAR 8   INTERNATIONAL WOMEN'S DAY
MAR 11 DAYLIGHT SAVING TIME BEGINS
MAR 17 ST. PATRICK'S DAY

MAR 18 MOTHERING SUNDAY (UK)
MAR 21 VERNAL EQUINOX 12:07 AM (GMT)
MAR 25 SUMMER TIME BEGINS (UK)

Obvious symmetry claims too much, I find, wearies the eye too soon and stultifies the imagination. Obvious symmetry usually closes the episode before it begins.

♦ ♦ ♦ Frank Lloyd Wright

Gregor S. Affleck House (1940), Bloomfield Hills, Michigan. This ultramodern house appeared in an advertisement for a "futuramic" Oldsmobile convertible. The ad drew a parallel between "the finest of contemporary architecture" and Oldsmobile's "dynamic design of the future."

monday

5   64

tuesday

6   65

wednesday

7   66

INTERNATIONAL WOMEN'S DAY

thursday

8   67

friday

9   68

saturday

10   69

s	m	t	w	t	f	s
				1	2	3
4	5	6	7	8	9	10
11	12	13	14	15	16	17
18	19	20	21	22	23	24
25	26	27	28	29	30	31

MARCH

DAYLIGHT SAVING TIME BEGINS

sunday

11   70

MARCH

monday

71   12 ☾

tuesday

72   13

wednesday

73   14

thursday

74   15

friday

75   16

saturday

76   17   ST. PATRICK'S DAY

sunday

77   18   MOTHERING SUNDAY (UK)

MARCH

_____

monday

● 19   78

_____

tuesday

20   79

_____

VERNAL EQUINOX 12:07 AM (GMT)

wednesday

21   80

_____

thursday

22   81

_____

friday

23   82

_____

saturday

24   83

_____

SUMMER TIME BEGINS (UK)

sunday

☽ 25   84

s	m	t	w	t	f	s
				1	2	3
4	5	6	7	8	9	10
11	12	13	14	15	16	17
18	19	20	21	22	23	24
25	26	27	28	29	30	31

MARCH

Human use and comfort should not be taxed to pay for any designer's idiosyncrasy.

◆　◆　◆　Frank Lloyd Wright

W. R. Heath House (1905), Buffalo, New York. Wright waged war on the double-hung window, ubiquitous at the turn of the century, specifying casement windows instead—often over the protests of clients and contractors.

MAR/APR

monday
26 85

tuesday
27 86

wednesday
28 87

thursday
29 88

friday
30 89

saturday
31 90

s	m	t	w	t	f	s
1	2	3	4	5	6	7
8	9	10	11	12	13	14
15	16	17	18	19	20	21
22	23	24	25	26	27	28
29	30					

APRIL

sunday
1 91

PALM SUNDAY

Architecture is the triumph of human imagination over materials, methods and men, to put man into possession of his own earth.

◆ ◆ ◆ Frank Lloyd Wright

Marin County Civic Center (1957–1962), San Rafael, California. Ever the modernist/iconoclast, Wright felt that the monumental elements borrowed from ancient Greece for use in civic architecture indicated that America simply had no style of its own. Designed to inspire its users, not just to impress them, Wright's Civic Center exemplifies his characteristic concerns: use of the latest technologies and materials, integration of building with landscape, and serving the people in the noblest way.

APRIL

SUNDAY	MONDAY	TUESDAY	WEDNESDAY	THURSDAY	FRIDAY	SATURDAY
1	2 ○	3	4	5	6	7
8	9	10 ☾	11	12	13	14
15	16	17 ●	18	19	20	21
22	23	24 ☽	25	26	27	28
29	30					

APR 1   PALM SUNDAY
APR 2   PASSOVER (BEGINS AT SUNSET)
APR 6   GOOD FRIDAY

APR 8   EASTER SUNDAY
APR 9   EASTER MONDAY (CANADA, UK)
APR 22   EARTH DAY

APRIL

monday

92   2 ○   PASSOVER (BEGINS AT SUNSET)

tuesday

93   3

wednesday

94   4

thursday

95   5

friday

96   6   GOOD FRIDAY

saturday

97   7

sunday

98   8   EASTER SUNDAY

APRIL

monday
9   99

EASTER MONDAY (CANADA, UK)

tuesday
10   100

wednesday
11   101

thursday
12   102

friday
13   103

saturday
14   104

sunday
15   105

s	m	t	w	t	f	s
1	2	3	4	5	6	7
8	9	10	11	12	13	14
15	16	17	18	19	20	21
22	23	24	25	26	27	28
29	30					

APRIL

Lighting may be made a part of the building itself. No longer any appliance or even appurtenance are needed. But all this may be made, really, architecture.

◆ ◆ ◆ Frank Lloyd Wright

Quintin Blair House (1952), Cody, Wyoming. Mitered-glass corners extend the views of interior spaces to the beautifully landscaped grounds. Filtered through graceful branches, the daylight breaks up into serene shadow patterns.

monday

16   106

tuesday

17   107

wednesday

18   108

thursday

19   109

friday

20   110

saturday

21   111

s	m	t	w	t	f	s
	1	2	3	4	5	6	7
8	9	10	11	12	13	14
15	16	17	18	19	20	21
22	23	24	25	26	27	28
29	30					

APRIL

EARTH DAY

sunday

22   112

> When a man wants to build a building he seeks an interpreter, does he not? He seeks some man who has the technique to express that thing which he himself desires but cannot do. So, should a man come to me for a building, he would be ready for me. It would be, what I could do, that he wanted.
>
> ◆ ◆ ◆   Frank Lloyd Wright

Lowell Walter House and River Pavilion (1948), Cedar Rock Park, Quasqueton, Iowa. Overlooking the Wapsipinicon River, Lowell and Agnes Walter's home is a Usonian with one big, indulgent difference: the 900-square-foot Garden Room, complete with a fireplace suitable for ox roasts. The Walter House—called "Cedar Rock"—is one of Wright's most comprehensive designs: nearly everything in it was created or chosen by the architect.

APRIL

monday

23   113

tuesday

☽ 24   114

wednesday

25   115

thursday

26   116

friday

27   117

saturday

28   118

s	m	t	w	t	f	s
1	2	3	4	5	6	7
8	9	10	11	12	13	14
15	16	17	18	19	20	21
22	23	24	25	26	27	28
29	30					

sunday

29   119

APRIL

APR/MAY

monday

120 30

tuesday

121 1

wednesday

122 2 ○

thursday

123 3

friday

124 4

saturday   CINCO DE MAYO

125 5

sunday

126 6

MAY

SUNDAY	◆	MONDAY	◆	TUESDAY	◆	WEDNESDAY	◆	THURSDAY	◆	FRIDAY	◆	SATURDAY
				1		2 ○		3		4		5
6		7		8		9		10 ☽		11		12
13		14		15		16 ●		17		18		19
20		21		22		23 ☽		24		25		26
27		28		29		30		31				

MAY 5   CINCO DE MAYO
MAY 7   BANK HOLIDAY (UK)
MAY 13 MOTHER'S DAY
MAY 19 ARMED FORCES DAY

MAY 21 VICTORIA DAY (CANADA)
MAY 28 MEMORIAL DAY OBSERVED
        BANK HOLIDAY (UK)
MAY 30 MEMORIAL DAY

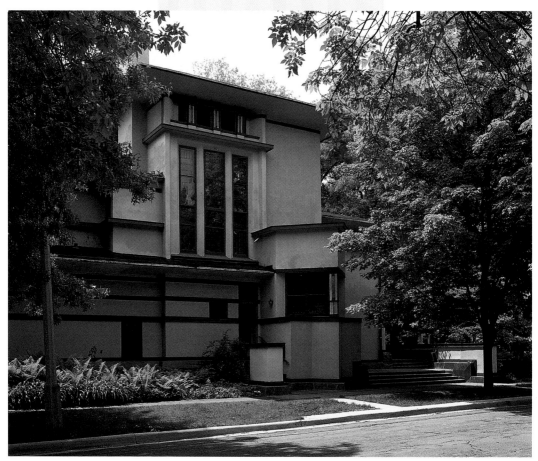

I added heights in the new buildings to no exaggerated established order nor to impress the beholder . . . but only to comfort the human being.
◆ ◆ ◆ Frank Lloyd Wright

Fricke-Martin House (1901), Oak Park, Illinois. Like the nearby William E. Martin House—and in sharp contrast to Wright's Prairie Style homes—this three-story residence emphasizes vertical lines.

MAY

BANK HOLIDAY (UK)

7 127

8 128

9 129

10 130

11 131

12 132

MOTHER'S DAY

13 133

s	m	t	w	t	f	s
		1	2	3	4	5
6	7	8	9	10	11	12
13	14	15	16	17	18	19
20	21	22	23	24	25	26
27	28	29	30	31		

MAY

MAY

monday

134 14

tuesday

135 15

wednesday

136 16 ●

thursday

137 17

friday

138 18

saturday

139 19   ARMED FORCES DAY

sunday

140 20

MAY

monday
VICTORIA DAY (CANADA)
21 141

tuesday
22 142

wednesday
☽ 23 143

thursday
24 144

friday
25 145

saturday
26 146

sunday
27 147

s	m	t	w	t	f	s
		1	2	3	4	5
6	7	8	9	10	11	12
13	14	15	16	17	18	19
20	21	22	23	24	25	26
27	28	29	30	31		

MAY

Architecture is born, not made—must consistently grow from within to whatever it becomes. Such forms as it takes must be spontaneous generation of materials, building methods and purpose.
◆ ◆ ◆ Frank Lloyd Wright

Roland Reisley House (1951), Pleasantville, New York. Wright personally designed three houses for the Pleasantville development; dozens more, also built in the Usonian style, share one hundred wooded acres and common facilities.

MAY/JUN

monday
28 148

MEMORIAL DAY OBSERVED

BANK HOLIDAY (UK)

tuesday
29 149

wednesday
30 150

MEMORIAL DAY

thursday
31 151

friday
01 152

saturday
2 153

sunday
3 154

s	m	t	w	t	f	s
					1	2
3	4	5	6	7	8	9
10	11	12	13	14	15	16
17	18	19	20	21	22	23
24	25	26	27	28	29	30

JUNE

Pope-Leighey House (1939), Mount Vernon, Virginia. Wright situated this Usonian carefully to allow its occupants maximum privacy; the home's "private" side is shown here. Typical of the Usonian concept, the Pope-Leighey House feels larger than its modest 1,200 square feet.

JUNE

SUNDAY	MONDAY	TUESDAY	WEDNESDAY	THURSDAY	FRIDAY	SATURDAY
					1 ○	2
3	4	5	6	7	8 ☾	9
10	11	12	13	14	15 ●	16
17	18	19	20	21	22 ☽	23
24	25	26	27	28	29	30 ○

JUN 8   FRANK LLOYD WRIGHT'S BIRTHDAY
JUN 14 FLAG DAY
JUN 17 FATHER'S DAY
JUN 21 SUMMER SOLSTICE 6:06 PM (GMT)

JUNE

monday

155 4

tuesday

156 5

wednesday

157 6

thursday

158 7

friday

159 8 ☾   FRANK LLOYD WRIGHT'S BIRTHDAY

saturday

160 9

sunday

161 10

JUNE

monday
11 162

tuesday
12 163

wednesday
13 164

thursday
14 165

FLAG DAY

friday
● 15 166

saturday
16 167

sunday
17 168

FATHER'S DAY

s	m	t	w	t	f	s
					1	2
3	4	5	6	7	8	9
10	11	12	13	14	15	16
17	18	19	20	21	22	23
24	25	26	27	28	29	30

JUNE

Frederick C. Robie House (1908–1910), Chicago, Illinois. Wright worked prolifically and brilliantly
in leaded glass, taking organic forms into the realm of abstraction or, as with these living room windows,
building patterns from pure geometric forms.

JUNE

SUMMER SOLSTICE 6:06 PM (GMT)

s	m	t	w	t	f	s
					1	2
3	4	5	6	7	8	9
10	11	12	13	14	15	16
17	18	19	20	21	22	23
24	25	26	27	28	29	30

JUNE

Lightness and strength! Steel the spider spinning a web within the cheap, molded material and wedded to it by pouring an inner core of cement after the blocks were set up.

◆ ◆ ◆ Frank Lloyd Wright

Louis Penfield House (1953), Willoughby Hills, Ohio. Wright rehabilitated the humble cinderblock with innovative construction technology and surface ornament. Strong verticals of wood and bold planes established by large windows make this an archetypally modernist structure.

JUN/JUL

monday
25 176

tuesday
26 177

wednesday
27 178

thursday
28 179

friday
29 180

saturday
○ 30 181

s	m	t	w	t	f	s
1	2	3	4	5	6	7
8	9	10	11	12	13	14
15	16	17	18	19	20	21
22	23	24	25	26	27	28
29	30	31				

JULY

sunday
1 182

CANADA DAY (CANADA)

Frank Lloyd Wright Home and Studio (1889–1898), Oak Park, Illinois. Wright's movement away from the highly ornate decorative style of the late nineteenth century can be seen in the contrast between the fretwork ceiling screen and the angular grace of the dining table and chairs—all made to his design.

JULY

SUNDAY	MONDAY	TUESDAY	WEDNESDAY	THURSDAY	FRIDAY	SATURDAY
1	2	3	4	5	6	7 ☾
8	9	10	11	12	13	14 ●
15	16	17	18	19	20	21
22 ☽	23	24	25	26	27	28
29	30 ○	31				

JUL 1   CANADA DAY (CANADA)
JUL 2   CANADA DAY OBSERVED
        (CANADA)
JUL 4   INDEPENDENCE DAY
JUL 12 BANK HOLIDAY (N. IRELAND)

JULY

monday _____
183   2

tuesday _____
184   3

wednesday _____
INDEPENDENCE DAY
185   4

thursday _____
186   5

friday _____
187   6

saturday _____
188   7 ☾

sunday _____
189   8

JULY

monday

9 190

tuesday

10 191

wednesday

11 192

thursday

12 193

BANK HOLIDAY (N. IRELAND)

friday

13 194

saturday

● 14 195

s	m	t	w	t	f	s
1	2	3	4	5	6	7
8	9	10	11	12	13	14
15	16	17	18	19	20	21
22	23	24	25	26	27	28
29	30	31				

JULY

sunday

15 196

Susan Lawrence Dana/Dana-Thomas House (1902–1904), Springfield, Illinois. Craftsman influence is present in the bedroom's decorative beams, dark wood, and built-in furnishings, but the airy proportions are Wright's.

JULY

monday

16   197

tuesday

17   198

wednesday

18   199

thursday

19   200

friday

20   201

saturday

21   202

s	m	t	w	t	f	s
1	2	3	4	5	6	7
8	9	10	11	12	13	14
15	16	17	18	19	20	21
22	23	24	25	26	27	28
29	30	31				

JULY

sunday

☽ 22   203

We all have the means to live free and independent, far apart—as we choose—still retaining all the social relationships and advantages we ever had, even to have them greatly amplified. No matter if we have houses a quarter of a mile apart.

♦ ♦ ♦ Frank Lloyd Wright

Roland Reisley House (1951), Pleasantville, New York. You won't find a more uplifting design for a carport. (Wright invented the concept and coined the term, by the way.) This house is still occupied by the Reisleys, who commissioned it with their honeymoon money.

JULY

s	m	t	w	t	f	s
1	2	3	4	5	6	7
8	9	10	11	12	13	14
15	16	17	18	19	20	21
22	23	24	25	26	27	28
29	30	31				

JULY

JUL/AUG

monday
211 30 ○

tuesday
212 31

wednesday
213 1

thursday
214 2

friday
215 3

saturday
216 4

sunday
217 5 ☽

AUGUST

SUNDAY	MONDAY	TUESDAY	WEDNESDAY	THURSDAY	FRIDAY	SATURDAY
			1	2	3	4
5 ☾	6	7	8	9	10	11
12 ●	13	14	15	16	17	18
19	20 ☽	21	22	23	24	25
26	27	28 ○	29	30	31	

AUG 6   CIVIC HOLIDAY (CANADA, MOST PROVINCES)
         BANK HOLIDAY (SCOTLAND)
AUG 27   BANK HOLIDAY (UK EXCEPT SCOTLAND)

AUGUST

monday
218
6

CIVIC HOLIDAY (CANADA, MOST PROVINCES)
BANK HOLIDAY (SCOTLAND)

tuesday
219
7

wednesday
220
8

thursday
221
9

friday
222
10

saturday
223
11

sunday
224
12 ●

AUGUST

13   225

tuesday

14   226

wednesday

15   227

thursday

16   228

friday

17   229

saturday

18   230

s	m	t	w	t	f	s
			1	2	3	4
5	6	7	8	9	10	11
12	13	14	15	16	17	18
19	20	21	22	23	24	25
26	27	28	29	30	31	

AUGUST

sunday

19   231

We must have as big a living room with as much
vista and garden coming in [as possible], with a
fireplace in it, and open bookshelves, . . . benches
and tables built-in.

◆ ◆ ◆ Frank Lloyd Wright

I. N. Hagan House, "Kentuck Knob" (1954), Chalkhill, Pennsylvania. Constructed on a hexagonal grid from stone and red cypress, the Hagans' home exemplifies organic architecture. From the outside it suggests a natural outcropping; from the inside, a well-lit and elegant cave.

AUGUST

☽ 20 232

21 233

22 234

23 235

24 236

25 237

s	m	t	w	t	f	s
			1	2	3	4
5	6	7	8	9	10	11
12	13	14	15	16	17	18
19	20	21	22	23	24	25
26	27	28	29	30	31	

AUGUST

26 238

*Architecture is life, or at least it is life itself
taking form and therefore it is the truest record
of life as it was lived in the world yesterday,
as it is lived today or ever will be lived.*
◆ ◆ ◆   Frank Lloyd Wright

Taliesin West (1937–1959), Scottsdale, Arizona. The rocky northern Sonoran Desert inspired the shapes and colors of Taliesin West. The complex is literally of the desert: local boulders, gathered and cemented together by apprentice architects, form most of its walls.

AUG/SEP

BANK HOLIDAY (UK EXCEPT SCOTLAND)

monday

27   239

tuesday

○ 28   240

wednesday

29   241

thursday

30   242

friday

31   243

saturday

1   244

sunday

2   245

s	m	t	w	t	f	s
						1
2	3	4	5	6	7	8
9	10	11	12	13	14	15
16	17	18	19	20	21	22
23	24	25	26	27	28	29
30						

SEPTEMBER

A modest house, this Usonian house, a dwelling place that has no feeling at all for the "grand" except as the house extends itself in the flat parallel to the ground. It will be a companion to the horizon.

◆ ◆ ◆ Frank Lloyd Wright

Pope-Leighey House (1939), Mount Vernon, Virginia. The Usonian concepts of architecture were developed to help put people of little means into wonderful houses. Wright built this one at a cost of $7,000 (including land) for a $50-a-week newspaperman.

SEPTEMBER

SUNDAY	MONDAY	TUESDAY	WEDNESDAY	THURSDAY	FRIDAY	SATURDAY
						1
2	3	4 ☾	5	6	7	8
9	10	11 ●	12	13	14	15
16	17	18	19 ☽	20	21	22
23	24	25	26 ○	27	28	29
30						

SEP 3   LABOR DAY (US, CANADA)

SEP 12   ROSH HASHANAH
(BEGINS AT SUNSET)

SEP 21   YOM KIPPUR (BEGINS AT SUNSET)

SEP 23   AUTUMNAL EQUINOX 9:51 AM (GMT)

SEPTEMBER

monday

246

3

LABOR DAY (US, CANADA)

tuesday

247

4 ☾

wednesday

248

5

thursday

249

6

friday

250

7

saturday

251

8

sunday

252

9

SEPTEMBER

ROSH HASHANAH (BEGINS AT SUNSET)

s	m	t	w	t	f	s
						1
2	3	4	5	6	7	8
9	10	11	12	13	14	15
16	17	18	19	20	21	22
23	24	25	26	27	28	29
30						

SEPTEMBER

It was not so easy to tell where pavements and walls left off and ground began. . . . Chimneys of the great stone fireplaces rose heavily . . . wherever there was a gathering place within, and there were many such places.

◆ ◆ ◆ Frank Lloyd Wright

Taliesin III (1911–1959), Spring Green, Wisconsin. The bodhisattva Guanyin, Chinese Buddhist deity of mercy, gazes serenely upon Taliesin's sloping lawn. At center right is the Tower Hill complex, now containing guest rooms; it housed chickens when Taliesin was a working farm.

monday

17 260

tuesday

18 261

wednesday

☽19 262

thursday

20 263

friday

YOM KIPPUR (BEGINS AT SUNSET)

21 264

saturday

22 265

s	m	t	w	t	f	s
						1
2	3	4	5	6	7	8
9	10	11	12	13	14	15
16	17	18	19	20	21	22
23	24	25	26	27	28	29
30			SEPTEMBER			

sunday

AUTUMNAL EQUINOX 9:51 AM (GMT)

23 266

*Shadows were the brushwork of the ancient
architect. Let the modern now work with light,
light diffused, light reflected, light refracted—
light for its own sake, shadows gratuitous.*

◆　◆　◆　　Frank Lloyd Wright

George Barton House (1903), Buffalo, New York. To Wright, the window was not just a means of getting light from one place to another: he saw windows as design opportunities for their own sake and as potential actors in a room's or building's rhythm and mood.

SEPTEMBER

monday

24 267

tuesday

25 268

wednesday

○ 26 269

thursday

27 270

friday

28 271

saturday

29 272

s	m	t	w	t	f	s
						1
2	3	4	5	6	7	8
9	10	11	12	13	14	15
16	17	18	19	20	21	22
23	24	25	26	27	28	29
30			SEPTEMBER			

sunday

30 273

I had an idea (it still seems to be my own) that the planes parallel to the earth in buildings identify themselves with the ground, do most to make the buildings belong to the ground.

◆   ◆   ◆   Frank Lloyd Wright

Karl A. Staley House (1950), North Madison, Ohio. This long, ground-hugging stone house features a surprise: on its "private" side, a wall of glass overlooks Lake Erie.

OCTOBER

SUNDAY	MONDAY	TUESDAY	WEDNESDAY	THURSDAY	FRIDAY	SATURDAY
	1	2	3 ☾	4	5	6
7	8	9	10	11 ●	12	13
14	15	16	17	18	19 ☽	20
21	22	23	24	25	26 ○	27
28	29	30	31			

OCT 8   COLUMBUS DAY OBSERVED
THANKSGIVING DAY (CANADA)
OCT 12 COLUMBUS DAY
OCT 24 UNITED NATIONS DAY

OCT 28 SUMMER TIME ENDS (UK)
OCT 31 HALLOWEEN

OCTOBER

monday
274
1

tuesday
275
2

wednesday
276
3 ☾

thursday
277
4

friday
278
5

saturday
279
6

sunday
280
7

OCTOBER

monday

8 281

COLUMBUS DAY OBSERVED

THANKSGIVING DAY (CANADA)

tuesday

9 282

wednesday

10 283

thursday

11 284

friday

12 285

COLUMBUS DAY

saturday

13 286

s	m	t	w	t	f	s
	1	2	3	4	5	6
7	8	9	10	11	12	13
14	15	16	17	18	19	20
21	22	23	24	25	26	27
28	29	30	31			

OCTOBER

sunday

14 287

We kept on inside with plenty of clean soft wood that could be left alone pretty much in plain surfaces. The stone, too, strong and protective inside, spoke for itself in certain piers and walls.

◆ ◆ ◆ Frank Lloyd Wright

Taliesin III (1911–1959), Spring Green, Wisconsin. Wright produced graceful, vigorous geometric designs and adapted them for murals, rugs, wall hangings and other textiles, metalwork, concrete blocks, lighting fixtures, etc.

OCTOBER

15 288

16 289

17 290

18 291

☽ 19 292

20 293

21 294

s	m	t	w	t	f	s
	1	2	3	4	5	6
7	8	9	10	11	12	13
14	15	16	17	18	19	20
21	22	23	24	25	26	27
28	29	30	31			

OCTOBER

Any good architect is by nature a physicist as a matter of fact, but as a matter of reality, as things are, he must be a philosopher and a physician.

◆ ◆ ◆ Frank Lloyd Wright

George Barton House (1903), Buffalo, New York. Quintessential Prairie Style in tawny brick, with art glass casement windows above a massively supported verandah.

OCTOBER

22   295

23   296

UNITED NATIONS DAY
24   297

25   298

○ 26   299

27   300

s	m	t	w	t	f	s
	1	2	3	4	5	6
7	8	9	10	11	12	13
14	15	16	17	18	19	20
21	22	23	24	25	26	27
28	29	30	31			

OCTOBER

SUMMER TIME ENDS (UK)
28   301

OCT/NOV

monday
302
29

tuesday
303
30

wednesday
304
31
HALLOWEEN

thursday
305
1

friday
306
2

saturday
307
3

sunday
308
4
DAYLIGHT SAVING TIME ENDS

NOVEMBER

SUNDAY	MONDAY	TUESDAY	WEDNESDAY	THURSDAY	FRIDAY	SATURDAY
				1 ☽	2	3
4	5	6	7	8	9 ●	10
11	12	13	14	15	16	17 ☽
18	19	20	21	22	23	24 ○
25	26	27	28	29	30	

NOV 4   DAYLIGHT SAVING TIME ENDS
NOV 11 VETERANS DAY
        REMEMBRANCE DAY (CANADA)

NOV 12 VETERANS DAY OBSERVED
NOV 22 THANKSGIVING DAY

NOVEMBER

monday
309   5

tuesday
310   6

wednesday
311   7

thursday
312   8

friday
313   9 ●

saturday
314   10

sunday
315   11

VETERANS DAY
REMEMBRANCE DAY (CANADA)

NOVEMBER

monday
12 316

VETERANS DAY OBSERVED

tuesday
13 317

wednesday
14 318

thursday
15 319

friday
16 320

saturday
☽ 17 321

s	m	t	w	t	f	s
				1	2	3
4	5	6	7	8	9	10
11	12	13	14	15	16	17
18	19	20	21	22	23	24
25	26	27	28	29	30	

NOVEMBER

sunday
18 322

When organic architecture is properly carried out no landscape is ever outraged by it but is always developed by it. The good building makes the landscape more beautiful than it was before the building was built.

◆   ◆   ◆   Frank Lloyd Wright

Gregor S. Affleck House (1940), Bloomfield Hills, Michigan. The Affleck home was built on sharply sloping ground; a creek was planned to flow beneath the cantilevered living room and feed a private pond.

NOVEMBER

monday
19 323

tuesday
20 324

wednesday
21 325

thursday
22 326

THANKSGIVING DAY

friday
23 327

saturday
○ 24 328

sunday
25 329

s	m	t	w	t	f	s
				1	2	3
4	5	6	7	8	9	10
11	12	13	14	15	16	17
18	19	20	21	22	23	24
25	26	27	28	29	30	

NOVEMBER

*What a man does—that he has. You may find
other things on him but they are not his.*
◆　◆　◆　Frank Lloyd Wright

Taliesin West (1937–1959), Scottsdale, Arizona. The theater ceiling recalls the canvas roofs of
Ocatillo, the camp Wright and his students built for their first stay in Arizona.

NOV/DEC

monday
26 330

tuesday
27 331

wednesday
28 332

thursday
29 333

friday
30 334

saturday
1 335

sunday
2 336

s	m	t	w	t	f	s
						1
2	3	4	5	6	7	8
9	10	11	12	13	14	15
16	17	18	19	20	21	22
23	24	25	26	27	28	29
30	31					

DECEMBER

Frederick C. Robie House (1908–1910), Chicago, Illinois. One of Wright's most famous commissions, the Robie House embodies the Prairie style with its sweeping horizontal lines and promise of cool, shady protection from the midwestern sun.

DECEMBER

SUNDAY	MONDAY	TUESDAY	WEDNESDAY	THURSDAY	FRIDAY	SATURDAY
						1 ☾
2	3	4	5	6	7	8
9 ●	10	11	12	13	14	15
16	17 ☽	18	19	20	21	22
23	24 ○	25	26	27	28	29
30	31 ☾					

DEC 4   HANUKKAH (BEGINS AT SUNSET)
DEC 22   WINTER SOLSTICE 6:08 AM (GMT)
DEC 25   CHRISTMAS DAY

DEC 26   BOXING DAY (CANADA, UK)
         KWANZAA BEGINS

DECEMBER

monday

337 3

tuesday

338 4

HANUKKAH (BEGINS AT SUNSET

wednesday

339 5

thursday

340 6

friday

341 7

saturday

342 8

sunday

343 9 ●

DECEMBER

monday

10 344

tuesday

11 345

wednesday

12 346

thursday

13 347

friday

14 348

saturday

15 349

s	m	t	w	t	f	s
						1
2	3	4	5	6	7	8
9	10	11	12	13	14	15
6	17	18	19	20	21	22
3	24	25	26	27	28	29
0	31					

DECEMBER

sunday

16 350

The interior space is the reality of the building. The room itself must come through or architecture has not arrived in the modern sense.

◆ ◆ ◆   Frank Lloyd Wright

John E. Christian House (1954), West Lafayette, Indiana. Wright's interiors tend to suggest their distinct constituent spaces—e.g., kitchen, dining room, gathering room—rather than to dictate them. This house, called Samara, has fifteen interrelated spaces if you include its sloping, artfully landscaped site.

DECEMBER

☽ 17   351

tuesday
18   352

wednesday
19   353

thursday
20   354

friday
21   355

saturday
22   356

WINTER SOLSTICE 6:08 AM (GMT)

sunday
23   357

s	m	t	w	t	f	s
						1
2	3	4	5	6	7	8
9	10	11	12	13	14	15
16	17	18	19	20	21	22
23	24	25	26	27	28	29
30	31					

DECEMBER

Proportion is nothing in itself. It is a matter of relation to environment modified always by every feature, exterior as well as interior.

◆   ◆   ◆   Frank Lloyd Wright

Peter A. Beachy House (1906), Oak Park, Illinois. Originally commissioned as a renovation and mostly built on an existing foundation, the Beachy House took form after years of wrangling and rejected design proposals. The exterior is quite unlike any other Wright work.

DECEMBER

CHRISTMAS DAY

BOXING DAY (CANADA, UK)

KWANZAA BEGINS

s	m	t	w	t	f	s
						1
2	3	4	5	6	7	8
9	10	11	12	13	14	15
16	17	18	19	20	21	22
23	24	25	26	27	28	29
30	31		DECEMBER			

DEC/JAN

monday

365 31 ☾

tuesday

1 1   NEW YEAR'S DAY

wednesday

2 2   BANK HOLIDAY (SCOTLAND)

thursday

3 3

friday

4 4

saturday

5 5

sunday

6 6

JANUARY

monday
7   7

tuesday
● 8   8

wednesday
9   9

thursday
10   10

friday
11   11

saturday
12   12

sunday
13   13

s	m	t	w	t	f	s
		1	2	3	4	5
6	7	8	9	10	11	12
13	14	15	16	17	18	19
20	21	22	23	24	25	26
27	28	29	30	31		

JANUARY

2008

JANUARY

s	m	t	w	t	f	s
		1	2	3	4	5
6	7	8	9	10	11	12
13	14	15	16	17	18	19
20	21	22	23	24	25	26
27	28	29	30	31		

FEBRUARY

s	m	t	w	t	f	s
					1	2
3	4	5	6	7	8	9
10	11	12	13	14	15	16
17	18	19	20	21	22	23
24	25	26	27	28	29	

MARCH

s	m	t	w	t	f	s
						1
2	3	4	5	6	7	8
9	10	11	12	13	14	15
16	17	18	19	20	21	22
$^{23}/_{30}$	$^{24}/_{31}$	25	26	27	28	29

APRIL

s	m	t	w	t	f	s
		1	2	3	4	5
6	7	8	9	10	11	12
13	14	15	16	17	18	19
20	21	22	23	24	25	26
27	28	29	30			

MAY

s	m	t	w	t	f	s
				1	2	3
4	5	6	7	8	9	10
11	12	13	14	15	16	17
18	19	20	21	22	23	24
25	26	27	28	29	30	31

JUNE

s	m	t	w	t	f	s
1	2	3	4	5	6	7
8	9	10	11	12	13	14
15	16	17	18	19	20	21
22	23	24	25	26	27	28
29	30					

2008

JULY

s	m	t	w	t	f	s
		1	2	3	4	5
6	7	8	9	10	11	12
13	14	15	16	17	18	19
20	21	22	23	24	25	26
27	28	29	30	31		

AUGUST

s	m	t	w	t	f	s
					1	2
3	4	5	6	7	8	9
10	11	12	13	14	15	16
17	18	19	20	21	22	23
24/31	25	26	27	28	29	30

SEPTEMBER

s	m	t	w	t	f	s
	1	2	3	4	5	6
7	8	9	10	11	12	13
14	15	16	17	18	19	20
21	22	23	24	25	26	27
28	29	30				

OCTOBER

s	m	t	w	t	f	s
			1	2	3	4
5	6	7	8	9	10	11
12	13	14	15	16	17	18
19	20	21	22	23	24	25
26	27	28	29	30	31	

NOVEMBER

s	m	t	w	t	f	s
						1
2	3	4	5	6	7	8
9	10	11	12	13	14	15
16	17	18	19	20	21	22
23/30	24	25	26	27	28	29

DECEMBER

s	m	t	w	t	f	s
	1	2	3	4	5	6
7	8	9	10	11	12	13
14	15	16	17	18	19	20
21	22	23	24	25	26	27
28	29	30	31			

2007 INTERNATIONAL HOLIDAYS

Following are the observed dates of major (bank-closing) holidays for selected countries in 2007. Islamic observances are subject to adjustment. Holidays for the US, UK, and Canada and major Jewish holidays appear on this calendar's grid pages. Pomegranate is not responsible for errors or omissions in this list. Users of this information should confirm dates with local sources before making international travel or business plans.

ARGENTINA

1 Jan	New Year's Day
2 Apr	Malvinas Islands Memorial
5 Apr	Holy Thursday
6 Apr	Good Friday
8 Apr	Easter
1 May	Labor Day
25 May	Revolution Day
18 Jun	Flag Day
9 Jul	Independence Day
20 Aug	General San Martín Anniversary
15 Oct	Día de la Raza
8 Dec	Immaculate Conception
25 Dec	Christmas

AUSTRALIA

1 Jan	New Year's Day
26 Jan	Australia Day
5 Mar	Labor Day (WA)
12 Mar	Labor Day (Vic) Eight Hours Day (Tas)
19 Mar	Canberra Day (ACT)
6 Apr	Good Friday
7–9 Apr	Easter Holiday
25 Apr	Anzac Day
7 May	Labor Day (Qld) May Day (NT)
4 Jun	Foundation Day (WA)
11 Jun	Queen's Birthday
6 Aug	Bank Holiday (NSW, NT)
1 Oct	Labor Day (NSW, ACT, SA)
25 Dec	Christmas
26 Dec	Boxing Day

BRAZIL

1 Jan	New Year's Day
20 Jan	São Sebastião Day (Rio de Janeiro)
25 Jan	São Paulo Anniversary (São Paulo)
19–20 Feb	Carnival
6 Apr	Good Friday
8 Apr	Easter
21 Apr	Tiradentes Day
1 May	Labor Day
7 Jun	Corpus Christi
9 Jul	State Holiday (São Paulo)
7 Sep	Independence Day
12 Oct	Our Lady of Aparecida
2 Nov	All Souls' Day
15 Nov	Proclamation of the Republic
20 Nov	Zumbi dos Palmares Day (Rio de Janeiro)
25 Dec	Christmas

CHINA (SEE ALSO HONG KONG)

1 Jan	New Year's Day
18–20 Feb	Lunar New Year
8 Mar	Women's Day
1–3 May	Labor Day Holiday
4 May	Youth Day
1 June	Children's Day
1 Aug	Army Day
1–3 Oct	National Holiday

FRANCE

1 Jan	New Year's Day
8–9 Apr	Easter Holiday
1 May	Labor Day
8 May	Armistice Day (WWII)
17 May	Ascension Day
27–28 May	Pentecost/Whitmonday
14 Jul	Bastille Day
15 Aug	Assumption Day
1 Nov	All Saints' Day
11 Nov	Armistice Day (WWI)
25 Dec	Christmas

GERMANY

1 Jan	New Year's Day
6 Jan	Epiphany*
6 Apr	Good Friday
8–9 Apr	Easter Holiday
1 May	Labor Day
17 May	Ascension Day
27–28 May	Pentecost/Whitmonday
7 Jun	Corpus Christi*
15 Aug	Assumption Day*
3 Oct	Unity Day
31 Oct	Reformation Day*
1 Nov	All Saints' Day*
21 Nov	Penance Day*
24–26 Dec	Christmas Holiday
31 Dec	New Year's Eve

*Observed only in some states

HONG KONG

1 Jan	New Year's Day
17–20 Feb	Lunar New Year
5 Apr	Ching Ming Festival
6–9 Apr	Easter Holiday
1 May	Labor Day
24 May	Buddha's Birthday
19 Jun	Tuen Ng Day
2 Jul	SAR Establishment Day
26 Sep	Mid-Autumn Festival
1 Oct	Chinese National Holiday
19 Oct	Chung Yeung Festival
25–26 Dec	Christmas Holiday

INDIA

20 Jan	Muharram (Islamic New Year)
26 Jan	Republic Day
31 Mar	Prophet Muhammad's Birthday Mahavir Jayanthi
6 Apr	Good Friday
2 May	Buddha Purnima
15 Aug	Independence Day
2 Oct	Mahatma Gandhi's Birthday
13 Oct	Ramzan Id (Eid-al-Fitr)
21 Oct	Dussehra
9 Nov	Diwali (Deepavali)
24 Nov	Guru Nanak's Birthday
20 Dec	Bakr-Id (Eid-al-Adha)
25 Dec	Christmas

Additional holidays to be declared

IRELAND

1 Jan	New Year's Day
17 Mar	St. Patrick's Day
8–9 Apr	Easter Holiday
7 May	May Holiday
4 Jun	June Holiday
6 Aug	August Holiday
29 Oct	October Holiday
25 Dec	Christmas
26 Dec	St. Stephen's Day

ISRAEL

4 Mar	Purim
3 Apr	First day of Pesach
9 Apr	Last day of Pesach
22 Apr	Memorial Day
23 Apr	Independence Day
23 May	Shavuot
24 Jul	Fast of Av
13–14 Sep	Rosh Hashanah
21–22 Sep	Yom Kippur
27 Sep	First day of Sukkot
4–5 Oct	Shemini Atzeret/Simhat Torah

ITALY

1 Jan	New Year's Day
6 Jan	Epiphany
8–9 Apr	Easter Holiday
25 Apr	Liberation Day
1 May	Labor Day
2 Jun	Republic Day
29 Jun	Sts. Peter and Paul (Rome)
15 Aug	Assumption Day
1 Nov	All Saints' Day
8 Dec	Immaculate Conception
25 Dec	Christmas
26 Dec	St. Stephen's Day

2007 INTERNATIONAL HOLIDAYS

JAPAN

1 Jan	New Year's Day
8 Jan	Coming of Age Day
12 Feb	National Foundation Day
21 Mar	Vernal Equinox Holiday
30 Apr	Greenery Day
3 May	Constitution Day
4 May	National Holiday
5 May	Children's Day
16 Jul	Marine Day
17 Sep	Respect for the Aged Day
24 Sep	Autumnal Equinox Holiday
8 Oct	Health and Sports Day
3 Nov	Culture Day
23 Nov	Labor Thanksgiving Day
24 Dec	Emperor's Birthday

KENYA

1 Jan	New Year's Day
6 Apr	Good Friday
8–9 Apr	Easter Holiday
1 May	Labor Day
1 Jun	Madaraka Day
10 Oct	Moi Day
13 Oct	Eid-al-Fitr
20 Oct	Kenyatta Day
12 Dec	Jamhuri Day
25 Dec	Christmas
26 Dec	Boxing Day

MEXICO

1 Jan	New Year's Day
5 Feb	Constitution Day
21 Mar	Benito Juárez's Birthday
5 Apr	Holy Thursday
6 Apr	Good Friday
8 Apr	Easter
1 May	Labor Day
5 May	Battle of Puebla
16 Sep	Independence Day
1 Nov	All Saints' Day
2 Nov	Day of the Dead
20 Nov	Revolution Day
12 Dec	Our Lady of Guadalupe
25 Dec	Christmas

NETHERLANDS

1 Jan	New Year's Day
6 Apr	Good Friday
8–9 Apr	Easter Holiday
30 Apr	Queen's Birthday
4 May	Remembrance Day
5 May	Liberation Day
17 May	Ascension Day
27–28 May	Pentecost/Whitmonday
25–26 Dec	Christmas Holiday

NEW ZEALAND

1–2 Jan	New Year's Holiday
22 Jan	Provincial Anniversary (Wellington)
29 Jan	Provincial Anniversary (Auckland)
6 Feb	Waitangi Day
6 Apr	Good Friday
8–9 Apr	Easter Holiday
25 Apr	Anzac Day
4 Jun	Queen's Birthday
22 Oct	Labor Day
16 Nov	Provincial Anniversary (Canterbury)
25 Dec	Christmas
26 Dec	Boxing Day

NORWAY

1 Jan	New Year's Day
1 Apr	Palm Sunday
5 Apr	Holy Thursday
6 Apr	Good Friday
8–9 Apr	Easter Holiday
1 May	Labor Day
17 May	Ascension Day Constitution Day
27–28 May	Pentecost/Whitmonday
25–26 Dec	Christmas Holiday

PUERTO RICO

1 Jan	New Year's Day
6 Jan	Three Kings Day (Epiphany)
8 Jan	Eugenio María de Hostos' Birthday
22 Mar	Emancipation Day
6 Apr	Good Friday
8 Apr	Easter
16 Apr	José de Diego's Birthday
16 Jul	Luís Muñoz Rivera's Birthday
25 Jul	Constitution Day
27 Jul	José Celso Barbosa's Birthday
8 Oct	Día de la Raza
19 Nov	Discovery of Puerto Rico
25 Dec	Christmas

All US federal holidays also observed.

RUSSIA

1–2 Jan	New Year's Holiday
7 Jan	Orthodox Christmas
23 Feb	Soldiers Day
8 Mar	International Women's Day
8 Apr	Orthodox Easter
1–2 May	Spring and Labor Day
9 May	Victory Day
12 Jun	Independence Day
7 Nov	Reconciliation Day
12 Dec	Constitution Day

SINGAPORE

1 Jan	New Year's Day
2 Jan	Hari Raya Haji (Eid-al-Adha)
18–20 Feb	Lunar New Year
6 Apr	Good Friday
8 Apr	Easter
1 May	Labor Day
31 May	Vesak Day (Buddha's Birthday)
9 Aug	National Day
13 Oct	Hari Raya Puasa (Eid-al-Fitr)

9 Nov	Deepavali
20 Dec	Hari Raya Haji (Eid-al-Adha)
25 Dec	Christmas

SOUTH AFRICA

1 Jan	New Year's Day
21 Mar	Human Rights Day
6 Apr	Good Friday
8 Apr	Easter
9 Apr	Family Day
27 Apr	Freedom Day
1 May	Labor Day
16 Jun	Youth Day
9 Aug	National Women's Day
24 Sep	Heritage Day
17 Dec	Day of Reconciliation
25 Dec	Christmas
26 Dec	Day of Goodwill

SPAIN

1 Jan	New Year's Day
6 Jan	Epiphany
19 Mar	St. Joseph's Day
5 Apr	Holy Thursday
6 Apr	Good Friday
8 Apr	Easter
1 May	Labor Day
25 Jul	St. James the Apostle Day
15 Aug	Assumption Day
12 Oct	National Holiday
1 Nov	All Saints' Day
6 Dec	Constitution Day
8 Dec	Immaculate Conception
25 Dec	Christmas

SWITZERLAND

1 Jan	New Year's Day
2 Jan	Berchtold's Day
6 Apr	Good Friday
8–9 Apr	Easter Holiday
17 May	Ascension Day
27–28 May	Pentecost/Whitmonday
1 Aug	National Day
25 Dec	Christmas
26 Dec	St. Stephen's Day

THAILAND

1 Jan	New Year's Day
2 Mar	Makha Bucha Day
6 Apr	Chakri Day
13–15 Apr	Songkran Festival
1 May	Labor Day Visakha Bucha Day (Buddha's Birthday)
7 May	Coronation Day
31 Jul	Buddhist Lent Day
13 Aug	Queen's Birthday
23 Oct	Chulalongkorn Day
5 Dec	King's Birthday
10 Dec	Constitution Day
31 Dec	New Year's Eve

INTERNATIONAL CALLING CODES/TIME DIFFERENCES

- From the United States, dial 011 (international access code), country code, city code, and local telephone number.
- Numbers listed alongside country names are country codes.
- Numbers listed alongside city names are city codes; an asterisk (*) means that no city code is needed.
- Numbers in parentheses indicate hourly differences from Pacific Standard Time. A range of numbers indicates a country with more than one time zone.
- Canada, US territories, and many Caribbean nations follow the North American Numbering Plan (dial 1 + 3-digit area code + local number) and are not listed here.

ALBANIA 355		(+9)
TIRANA 4		
ALGERIA 213		(+9)
ALGIERS 2		
ARGENTINA 54		(+5)
BUENOS AIRES 11		
CÓRDOBA 351		
SANTA FÉ 342		
ARMENIA 374		(+12)
YEREVAN 10		
ARUBA 297		(+4)
ALL CITIES 8		
AUSTRALIA 61		(+16–18)
ADELAIDE 8		
BRISBANE 7		
CANBERRA 2		
MELBOURNE 3		
PERTH 8		
SYDNEY 2		
AUSTRIA 43		(+9)
SALZBURG 662		
VIENNA 1		
BANGLADESH 880		(+14)
CHITTAGONG 31		
DHAKA 2		
BELGIUM 32		(+9)
ANTWERP 3		
BRUSSELS 2		
GHENT 9		
BOLIVIA 591		(+4)
LA PAZ 2		
SANTA CRUZ 3		
BOSNIA-HERZEGOVINA . . 387		(+9)
SARAJEVO 33		
BRAZIL 55		(+3–6)
BRASÍLIA 61		
RIO DE JANEIRO 21		
SALVADOR 71		
SÃO PAULO 11		
BULGARIA 359		(+10)
SOFIA 2		
CAMBODIA 855		(+15)
PHNOM PENH 23		
CAMEROON 237*		(+9)
CENTRAL AFRICAN REPUBLIC 236*		(+9)
CHILE 56		(+4)
CONCEPCIÓN 41		
SANTIAGO 2		
VALPARAÍSO 32		

CHINA 86		(+16)
BEIJING 10		
CANTON (GUANGZHOU) 20		
FUZHOU 591		
SHANGHAI 21		
COLOMBIA 57		(+3)
BOGOTÁ 1		
CALI 2		
MEDELLÍN 4		
CONGO 242*		(+9)
CONGO, DEMOCRATIC		
REPUBLIC OF 243		(+9–10)
KINSHASA 1		
COSTA RICA 506*		(+2)
CROATIA 385		(+9)
DUBROVNIK 20		
ZAGREB 1		
CUBA 53		(+3)
GUANTÁNAMO BAY NAVAL		
BASE (FROM US ONLY) 99		
HAVANA 7		
CYPRUS 357		(+10)
NICOSIA 22		
CZECH REPUBLIC 420		(+9)
PRAGUE 2		
DENMARK 45*		(+9)
ECUADOR 593		(+3)
GUAYAQUIL 4		
QUITO 2		
EGYPT 20		(+10)
ALEXANDRIA 3		
CAIRO 2		
EL SALVADOR 503*		(+2)
ESTONIA 372		(+10)
TALLINN 6		
ETHIOPIA 251		(+11)
ADDIS ABABA 1		
FIJI 679* . . . .(+20)		
FINLAND 358		(+10)
HELSINKI 9		
FRANCE 33		(+9)
BORDEAUX 5		
MARSEILLE 491		
NICE 4		
PARIS 1		
REIMS 3		
ROUEN 2		
TOULOUSE 5		
FRENCH ANTILLES 590*		(+4)
FRENCH POLYNESIA . . . 689*		(-1–2)
(MOOREA AND TAHITI)		
GEORGIA 995		(+12)
TBILISI 32		
GERMANY 49		(+9)
BERLIN 30		
FRANKFURT 69		
HAMBURG 40		
MUNICH 89		
GIBRALTAR 350*		(+9)
GREECE 30		(+10)
ATHENS 1		
IRÁKLION (CRETE) 81		
GUATEMALA 502		(+2)
GUATEMALA CITY 2		

HAITI 509*		(+3)
HONDURAS 504*		(+2)
HONG KONG 852*		(+16)
HUNGARY 36		(+9)
BUDAPEST 1		
DEBRECEN 52		
ICELAND 354*		(+8)
INDIA 91		(+13.5)
BANGALORE 80		
BOMBAY (MUMBAI) 22		
CALCUTTA 33		
MADRAS 44		
NEW DELHI 11		
INDONESIA 62		(+15–17)
JAKARTA 21		
IRAN 98		(+11.5)
ESFAHAN 311		
SHIRAZ 711		
TEHRAN 211		
IRAQ 964		(+11)
BAGHDAD 1		
BASRA 40		
KIRKUK 50		
MOSUL 60		
IRELAND 353		(+8)
CORK 21		
DUBLIN 1		
ISRAEL 972		(+10)
HAIFA 4		
JERUSALEM 2		
TEL AVIV 3		
ITALY 39		(+9)
FLORENCE 055		
GENOA 010		
MILAN 02		
NAPLES 081		
ROME 06		
VENICE 041		
IVORY COAST 225*		(+8)
JAPAN 81		(+17)
KYOTO 75		
TOKYO 3		
YOKOHAMA 45		
JORDAN 962		(+10)
AMMAN 6		
KARAK 3		
KENYA 254		(+11)
MOMBASA 11		
NAIROBI 2		
N. KOREA 850		(+17)
S. KOREA 82		(+17)
KWANGJU 62		
PUSAN 51		
SEOUL 2		
TAEGU 53		
KUWAIT 965*		(+11)
LAOS 856		(+15)
VIENTIANE 21		
LATVIA 371		(+10)
RIGA 2		
LEBANON 961		(+10)
BEIRUT 1		
LIBERIA 231*		(+8)

INTERNATIONAL CALLING CODES/TIME DIFFERENCES

LIBYA . . . . 218 (+10)
  TRIPOLI 21
LIECHTENSTEIN . . . . . . 423* (+9)
LITHUANIA . . . . 370 (+10)
  KAUNAS 37
LUXEMBOURG . . . . 352* (+9)
MACAU . . . . 853* (+16)
MACEDONIA . . . . 389 (+9)
MALAYSIA . . . . 60 (+16)
  IPOH 5
  KUALA LUMPUR 3
MEXICO . . . . 52 (+0–2)
  ACAPULCO 744
  CABO SAN LUCAS 624
  CANCÚN 998
  CIUDAD JUÁREZ 656
  ENSENADA 646
  GUADALAJARA 33
  LA PAZ 612
  MAZATLÁN 669
  MEXICALI 686
  MEXICO CITY 55
  MONTERREY 81
  TIJUANA 664
  VERACRUZ 229
MONACO . . . . 377* (+9)
MOROCCO . . . . 212 (+8)
  MARRAKECH 44
  RABAT 37
MOZAMBIQUE . . . . 258 (+10)
  MAPUTO 1
MYANMAR . . . . 95 (+14.5)
  RANGOON (YANGON) 1
NAMIBIA . . . . 264 (+9)
  WINDHOEK 61
NEPAL . . . . 977 (+14)
  KATHMANDU 1
NETHERLANDS . . . . 31 (+9)
  AMSTERDAM 20
  THE HAGUE (DEN HAAG) 70
  ROTTERDAM 10
NETHERLANDS ANTILLES . . 599 (+4)
  CURAÇAO 9
  ST. MAARTEN 5
NEW ZEALAND . . . . 64 (+20–21)
  AUCKLAND 9
  CHRISTCHURCH 3
  WELLINGTON 4
NICARAGUA . . . . 505 (+2)
  LEÓN 311
  MANAGUA 2
NIGERIA . . . . 234 (+9)
  LAGOS 1
NORWAY . . . . 47* (+9)
PAKISTAN . . . . 92 (+13)
  ISLAMABAD 51
  KARACHI 21
  LAHORE 42
PANAMA . . . . 507* (+3)
PARAGUAY . . . . 595 (+4)
  ASUNCIÓN 21
  CONCEPCIÓN 31

PERU . . . . 51 (+3)
  AREQUIPA 54
  LIMA 1
PHILIPPINES . . . . 63 (+16)
  BACOLOD 34
  CEBU CITY 32
  DAVAO 82
  ILOILO CITY 33
  MANILA 2
POLAND . . . . 48 (+9)
  GDANSK 58
  KRAKOW 12
  WARSAW 22
PORTUGAL . . . . 351 (+8)
  LISBON 21
ROMANIA . . . . 40 (+10)
  BUCHAREST 21
RUSSIA . . . . 7 (+10–20)
  MOSCOW 095
  ST. PETERSBURG 812
SAUDI ARABIA . . . . . . 966 (+11)
  JEDDAH 2
  MECCA (MAKKAH) 2
  RIYADH 1
SENEGAL . . . . 221* (+8)
SERBIA AND MONTENEGRO 381 (+9)
  BELGRADE 11
  CETINJE 86
SINGAPORE . . . . 65* (+16)
SLOVAKIA . . . . 421 (+9)
  BRATISLAVA 2
SLOVENIA . . . . 386 (+9)
  LJUBLJANA 1
  MARIBOR 2
SOUTH AFRICA . . . . 27 (+10)
  BLOEMFONTEIN 51
  CAPE TOWN 21
  DURBAN 31
  JOHANNESBURG 11
  PRETORIA 12
SPAIN . . . . 34 (+9)
  BARCELONA 93
  GRANADA 958
  MADRID 91
  PALMA DE MALLORCA 971
  PAMPLONA 948
  SEVILLE 95
  VALENCIA 96
SRI LANKA . . . . 94 (+14)
  COLUMBO CENTRAL 1
SURINAME . . . . 597* (+5)
SWEDEN . . . . 46 (+9)
  MALMO 40
  STOCKHOLM 8
SWITZERLAND . . . . 41 (+9)
  BASEL 61
  BERNE 31
  GENEVA 22
  LAUSANNE 21
  LUCERNE 41
  ZÜRICH 1
SYRIA . . . . 963 (+10)
  DAMASCUS 11

TAIWAN . . . . 886 (+16)
  KAO-HSIUNG 7
  TAINAN 6
  TAIPEI 2
TANZANIA . . . . 255 (+11)
  DAR ES SALAAM 22
  TANGA 27
THAILAND . . . . 66 (+15)
  BANGKOK 2
  CHANTHABURI 39
TUNISIA . . . . 216 (+9)
  BIZERTE 2
  TUNIS 1
TURKEY . . . . 90 (+10)
  ANKARA 312
  ISTANBUL
    ASIAN 216
    EUROPEAN 212
UGANDA . . . . 256 (+11)
  ENTEBBE 42
  KAMPALA 41
UKRAINE . . . . 380 (+10)
  DONETSK 62(2)
  KIEV 44
  LVOV 32(2)
UNITED ARAB EMIRATES. . .971 (+12)
  ABU DHABI 2
  AJMAN 6
  AL AIN 3
  FUJAIRAH 9
UNITED KINGDOM . . . . . . 44 (+8)
  BELFAST 28
  BIRMINGHAM 121
  CARDIFF 29
  EDINBURGH 131
  GLASGOW 141
  LIVERPOOL 151
  LONDON 20
  MANCHESTER 161
  SOUTHAMPTON 23
URUGUAY . . . . 598 (+5)
  CANELONES 332
  MERCEDES 532
  MONTEVIDEO 2
VATICAN CITY . . . . 39 (+9)
  ALL POINTS 6
VENEZUELA . . . . 58 (+4)
  CARACAS 212
  MARACAIBO 261
  MARACAY 243
  VALENCIA 241
VIETNAM . . . . 84 (+15)
  HANOI 4
  HO CHI MINH CITY 8
YEMEN . . . . 967 (+11)
  ADEN 2
  SANA'A 1
  ZABID 3
ZAMBIA . . . . 260 (+10)
  LUSAKA 1
ZIMBABWE . . . . 263 (+10)
  HARARE 4

NOTES

PERSONAL INFORMATION

name _____

address _____

city _____ state _____ zip _____

phone _____

cell/pgr _____ fax _____

e-mail _____

in case of emergency, please notify:

name _____

address _____

city _____ state _____ zip _____

phone _____

physician's name _____

physician's phone _____

health insurance company _____

plan number _____

allergies _____

other _____

driver's license number _____

car insurance company _____

policy number _____